Barn Owl

by Kathryn Camisa

Consultant: Thane Maynard, Director
Cincinnati Zoo and Botanical Garden
Cincinnati, Ohio

BEARPORT
PUBLISHING

New York, New York

Credits

Cover, © davehuntphotography/Shutterstock; TOC, © muratart/Shutterstock; 4–5, © M-Reinhardt/Shutterstock; 6L, © Alex Coan/Shutterstock; 6R, © absolutimages/Shutterstock; 7, © guentermanaus/Shutterstock; 8, © Nick Biemans/Shutterstock; 9, © Melanie Lindenthal/Barn Owl Trust; 10L, © Ondrej Prosicky/Shutterstock; 10R, © johnrich/iStock; 11, © Yorkiesteve/Dreamstime; 12, © JillLang/iStock; 13TR, © Thanit Weerawan/Shutterstock; 13TL, © Thanit Weerawan/Shutterstock; 13BR, © Thanit Weerawan/Shutterstock; 13BL, © Thanit Weerawan/Shutterstock; 14–15, © Mark Medcalf/Shutterstock; 15R, © JBKC/Shutterstock; 16, © Maureen Perez/Shutterstock; 17T, © Eric Isselee/Shutterstock; 17M, © charliebishop/iStock; 17B, © sonsam/Shutterstock; 18, © Michael Könen/Thinkstock; 19, © KOO/Shutterstock; 21, © Matt Cuda/Shutterstock; 22T, © Mauricio S. Ferreira/Shutterstock; 22M, © Ed Schneider/Shutterstock; 22B, © Alan Tunnicliffe/Shutterstock; 23TL, Michael Könen/iStock; 23TR, © Cloebudgie/Thinkstock; 23BL, © neil hardwick/Shutterstock; 23BR, © Dirk Wegman/Shutterstock.

Publisher: Kenn Goin
Senior Editor: Joyce Tavolacci
Creative Director: Spencer Brinker
Design: Debrah Kaiser
Photo Researcher: Olympia Shannon

Library of Congress Cataloging-in-Publication Data

Names: Camisa, Kathryn, author.
Title: Barn owl / by Kathryn Camisa.
Description: New York, New York : Bearport Publishing, [2016] | Series: Weird but cute | Audience: Ages 4–8. | Includes bibliographical references and index.
Identifiers: LCCN 2015037212| ISBN 9781943553273 (library binding) | ISBN 1943553270 (library binding)
Subjects: LCSH: Barn owl—Juvenile literature.
Classification: LCC QL696.S85 C37 2016 | DDC 598.9/7—dc23
LC record available at http://lccn.loc.gov/2015037212

For more information, write to Bearport Publishing Company, Inc., 45 West 21st Street, Suite 3B, New York, New York 10010. Printed in the United States of America.

10 9 8 7 6 5 4 3 2 1

Contents

What's this weird
but cute animal?

It's a
barn owl.

Heart-
shaped
face!

Long wings!

5

How big is a barn owl?

It's about the size of
an adult cat.

Yet it only weighs as
much as a kitten!

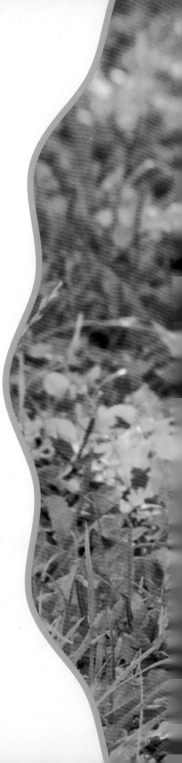

Male barn owls are smaller than female barn owls.

Barn owls have long wings.

Their wings are covered with soft feathers.

When the owls flap their wings, they hardly make a sound!

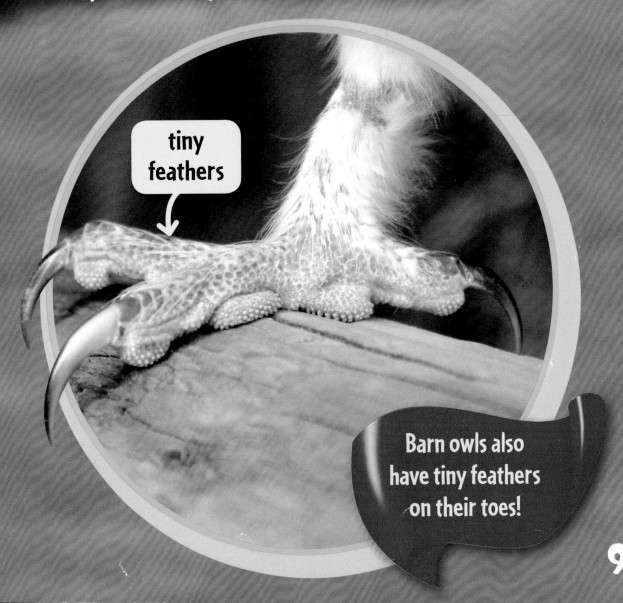

tiny feathers

Barn owls also have tiny feathers on their toes!

9

During the day, barn owls sleep.

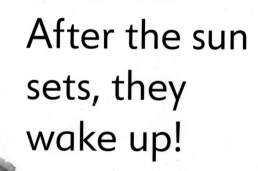

After the sun sets, they wake up!

Then, they soar through the air looking for food.

Some barn owls like to sleep in barns. This is how they got their name!

A barn owl uses its big, round eyes to see in the dark.

Yet the bird can't move its eyes!

To see, it turns its head from side to side.

Owls can turn their heads almost all the way around!

13

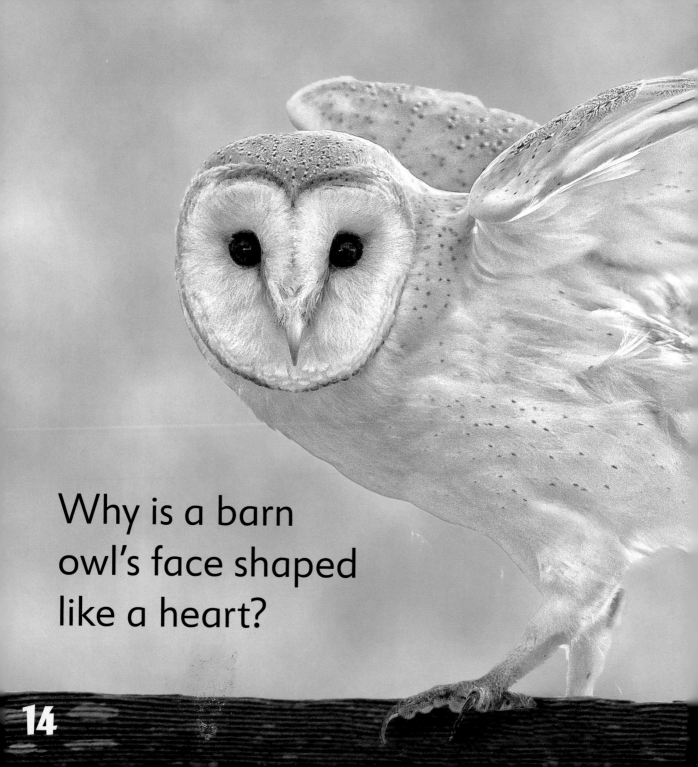

Why is a barn
owl's face shaped
like a heart?

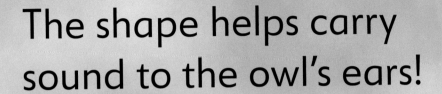

The shape helps carry sound to the owl's ears!

Let's hear it! Barn owls have great hearing. They use their hearing to find small animals hiding in the grass.

Barn owls have sharp claws.

These claws are called **talons**.

Owls use their talons to catch **prey**.

prey

vole

Barn owls eat mostly mice and small animals called voles.

Gulp, gulp! Barn owls swallow their prey whole.

mouse

They can't **digest** some parts of the animals they eat, though.

So their bodies turn these bits into **pellets**.

Then the birds cough up the pellets.

fur

skin

bone

An owl pellet is about the size of a thumb. It contains bones, skin, and fur.

What sound does
a barn owl make?

It doesn't make
a hoot!

Instead, it hisses,
grunts, and shrieks.

Listen for one
in the night sky!

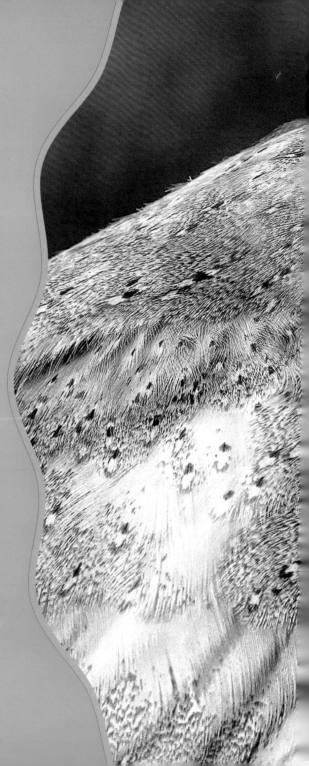

A barn owl will open and close its beak when it's surprised.

More Weird Owls

Burrowing Owl
This tiny owl nests underground. It bobs its head up and down and makes strange clucking and chattering sounds.

Elf Owl
The elf owl is the world's smallest owl. It stands about 6 inches (15 cm) tall. If it's captured, it will play dead!

White-Faced Scops Owl
This owl has huge orange eyes that can be seen from far away. When the owl is hiding from enemies, it closes its eyes and shows only its feathery eyelids to blend in with its surroundings.

Glossary

digest (dye-JEST) to break down food inside the body

pellets (PEL-its) small balls of food that cannot be broken down

prey (PRAY) animals that are hunted and eaten by other animals

talons (TAL-uhnz) the sharp claws of a hunting bird

Index

Read More

Phillips, Dee. *Burrowing Owl's Hideaway (The Hole Truth! Underground Animal Life).* New York: Bearport (2015).

Rissman, Rebecca. *Barn Owls: Nocturnal Hunters.* North Mankato, MN: Heinemann-Raintree (2015).

Learn More Online

To learn more about barn owls, visit
www.bearportpublishing.com/WeirdButCute

About the Author

Kathryn Camisa rarely sees owls near her home in New York City. So she flew to Scotland to meet a barn owl with a heart-shaped face that shrieks and screeches but never hoots.